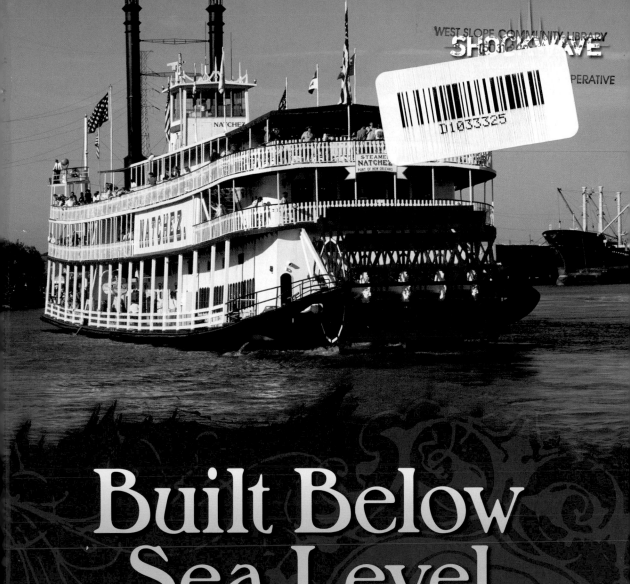

Built Below Sea Level

NEW ORLEANS

Laura Layton Strom

children's press®

An imprint of Scholastic Inc.

NEW YORK • TORONTO • LONDON • AUCKLAND • SYDNEY
MEXICO CITY • NEW DELHI • HONG KONG
DANBURY, CONNECTICUT

Library of Congress Cataloging-in-Publication Data
Strom, Laura Layton, 1962-
Built below sea level : New Orleans / by Laura Layton Strom.
p. cm. -- (Shockwave)
Includes index.
ISBN-10: 0-531-17746-7 (lib. bdg.)
ISBN-13: 978-0-531-17746-4 (lib. bdg.)
ISBN-10: 0-531-18774-8 (pbk.)
ISBN-13: 978-0-531-18774-6 (pbk.)

1. New Orleans (La.)--History--Juvenile literature. 2. New Orleans
(La.)--Social life and customs--Juvenile literature. 3. New Orleans
(La.)--Geography--Juvenile literature. 4. Hurricane Katrina,
2005--Juvenile literature. 5. New Orleans (La.)--Environmental
conditions--Juvenile literature. I. Title. II. Series.

F379.N557S77 2008
976.3'35--dc22
2007010059

Published in 2008 by Children's Press, an imprint of Scholastic Inc.,
557 Broadway, New York, New York 10012
www.scholastic.com

08 09 10 11 12 13 14 15 16 17
10 9 8 7 6 5 4 3 2 1

Printed in China through Colorcraft Ltd., Hong Kong

Author: Laura Layton Strom
Editors: Mary Atkinson and Laura Layton Strom
Designer: Avon Willis
Photo Researcher: Sarah Matthewson

Photographs by: Getty Images (cover; alligator release, p. 19; flooded suburb, p. 21;
rescued pets, p. 27); **Jennifer and Brian Lupton** (girl, p. 31); **NOAA/NESDIS: National
Environmental Satellite, Data and Information Service** (satellite image of Hurricane
Katrina, p. 23); **Photolibrary** (p. 1; p. 8; pp. 10–11; p. 15; nutria, p. 19; traffic jam,
pp. 22–23; family celebrating Mardi Gras, p. 28; evacuation sign, p. 29); **Tranz/Corbis**
(p. 5; pp. 6–7; pp. 12–13; p. 14; pp. 16–18; p. 20; graveyard, p. 21; pp. 24–26; family
cleaning up, p. 27; boy and placard, pp. 28–29; p. 29; construction site, pp. 30–31)

 All illustrations and other photographs © Weldon Owen Education Inc.

CONTENTS

bayou *(BYE oo)* a stream or body of water that runs slowly through a swamp and leads to or from a lake or a river

Cajun *(KAY juhn)* a person who is descended from French-speaking people who left Canada for Louisiana in the 1700s; to do with the cooking or the culture of Cajun people

gumbo a soup often made with okra and seafood. It is a speciality of New Orleans.

levee a natural or human-made embankment alongside a river, which prevents flooding

Mardi Gras the name, meaning Fat Tuesday in French, — 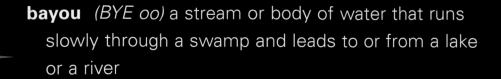 for a New Orleans festival of parades and parties

sea level the level of the surface of the ocean

· ·

For easy reference, see Wordmark on back flap.
For additional vocabulary, see Glossary on page 32.

The word *bayou* sounds like "bye oo." It has gone through several different changes in spelling since its first use in the eighteenth century, trying to get the sound right! Some of these include *bayoo, byo, bayyou.*

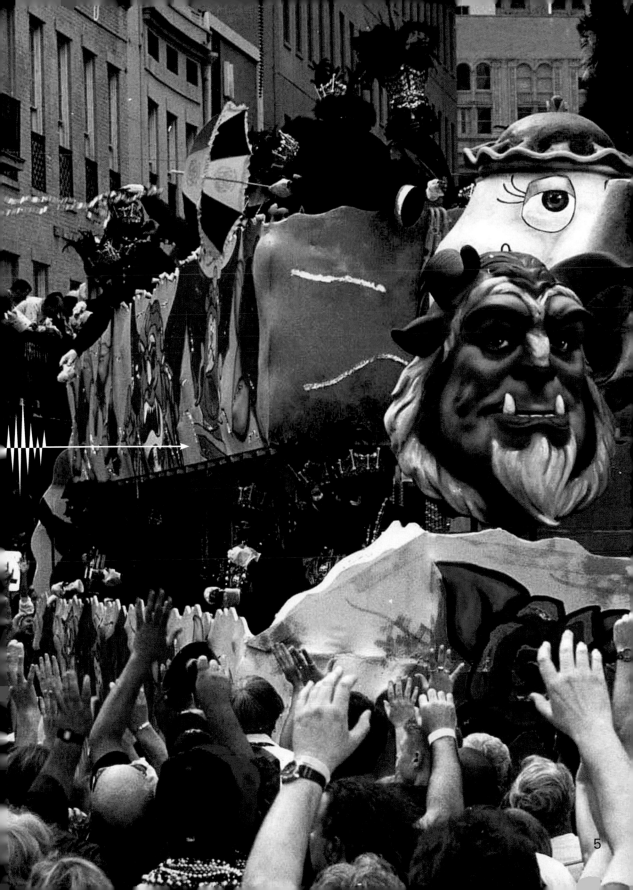

If you ever get the chance, take a tour through the swamps of southern Louisiana. There, quiet back roads wind through swampy **bayous**. After sunset, a foggy mist is likely to settle. Mosquitoes become the enemy of the unprotected. The eerie, murky water ripples with flashes from alligator eyes.

Take a tour by day and you may see the same alligators sunning themselves on rocks. Tour guides might throw raw chicken into the water so observers can watch the 'gators feed. It is hard to believe that this swamp-soaked land is just minutes from a city – a city built below **sea level**. The city is New Orleans.

At nightfall, some swamps of the southeastern United States are lit with the reflective eyes of floating alligators.

New Orleans sits on a **crescent** of land. It is nestled along the Mississippi River. North of the city is the massive Lake Pontchartrain. The city is surrounded by water, and it lies on a bed of land on top of water.

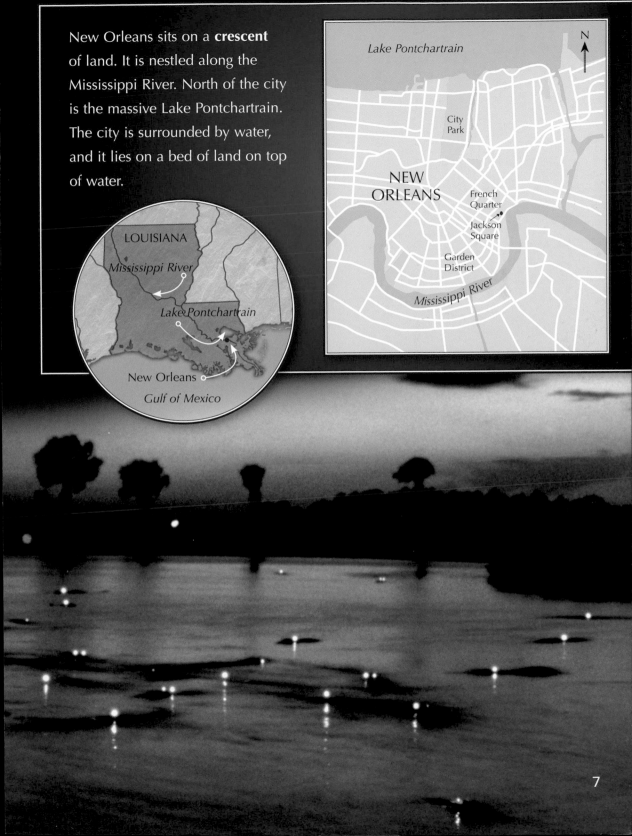

Lake Pontchartrain

N

City Park

NEW ORLEANS

French Quarter

Jackson Square

Garden District

Mississippi River

LOUISIANA

Mississippi River

Lake Pontchartrain

New Orleans

Gulf of Mexico

From Swamp to City

Native Americans were the original **inhabitants** of the New Orleans area. A Spanish explorer named Hernando de Soto was the first European to discover the Mississippi River, in 1541. In 1682, a Frenchman, Sieur de La Salle, sailed down the river from Canada and claimed land along the Mississippi. He named the land Louisiana after his king, Louis XIV. In 1718, another Frenchman, Sieur de Bienville, chose the site for New Orleans. He was the founder of the city.

Hernando de Soto was greeted warmly by this group of Native Americans.

NEW ORLEANS TIME LINE

1541	1682	1718	1763	1763
De Soto discovers Mississippi River.	De La Salle claims Louisiana for Louis XIV.	First settlement in New Orleans founded by Sieur de Bienville.	French and Indian War ends.	Treaty of Paris gives Louisiana to the Spanish king, Charles III.

HOT-POTATO OWNERSHIP

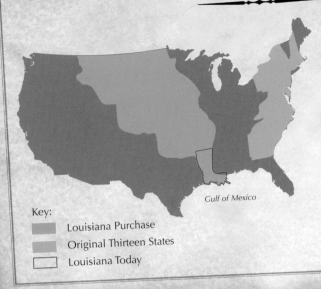

Key:
- Louisiana Purchase
- Original Thirteen States
- Louisiana Today

Gulf of Mexico

Louisiana passed from French control to Spanish control, and then back to French control again. Finally, in 1803, it was sold to the United States for about $15 million. This land was part of what was called the Louisiana Purchase. In 1812, Louisiana joined the United States as its eighteenth state.

New Orleans might not have looked at first glance like a great place to settle. It was hot, **humid**, and swampy. The mosquitoes were fierce. Early settlers report that the native people were not always welcoming. France was also dumping its prisoners in New Orleans. In spite of this, the city prospered. Its position on the river and the Gulf of Mexico made it a great port for trade.

This time line will be really useful. I can refer back to it to check information as I read the next few pages, or use it to review what I have learned.

1800	1803	1812	1814	1815
Louisiana passes from Spain back to France.	Louisiana and other territory sold to the United States as the Louisiana Purchase.	Louisiana becomes eighteenth state.	On December 24, the Treaty of Ghent supposedly ends the War of 1812.	Americans win Battle of New Orleans on January 8, and the War of 1812 ends.

FIGHTING FOR NEW ORLEANS

New Orleans has an important place in United States history. During the War of 1812, the city was a raging battlefield. The war had been fought off and on for more than two years. The Americans were defending their claims to land won in the American Revolution (1775–1783). In January 1815, the British attacked New Orleans. However, the British troops underestimated the Americans.

The British were a red-coated troop of professional soldiers. The Americans were a ragged group of citizens, pirates, and Native Americans. However, led by General Andrew Jackson, the Americans won a stunning victory. More than 2,000 British died, while the Americans lost only eight men. **Ironically**, a peace treaty had been signed some weeks before, but word traveled slowly in those days. The Battle of New Orleans made a hero of Andrew Jackson. In 1828, he was elected president of the United States.

SHOCKER

Before the Civil War, river trade helped to make New Orleans the richest city in the South. With the coming of the railroads, river trade became less important. New Orleans became the poorest city in the country!

New Orleans was named after Orleans, a city in France. There are many cities, states, and even whole countries that are named after other places. For example, the state of New Mexico is named after the country of Mexico.

From Pirate to Patriot

A fierce pirate named Jean Lafitte helped the Americans win the Battle of New Orleans. Lafitte and his crew had great knowledge of the local ocean and waterways. Lafitte also had a large stash of weapons and military supplies. Interestingly, the British were the first to ask Lafitte for his help. But Jackson was one step ahead. He offered Lafitte forgiveness for past pirating offenses if he helped the Americans. Lafitte became a hero. There is now a national historic park named after him in New Orleans!

MULTICULTURAL GUMBO

New Orleans is a rich "**gumbo**" of many cultures, granting it a special status among American cities. Its multicultural atmosphere has long been an attraction for immigrant groups. The city is an **integrated** mix of French, Spanish, Irish, Italian, African, Native-American, and Jewish influences. The **Cajuns**, originally from French-speaking Canada, add their culture to the gumbo as well.

New Orleans food is famously spicy and **pungent**. It is unlike that of any other place in the United States. Similarly, the music of New Orleans is a rich mixture of styles and traditions.

Members of the Cajun community dance at the annual Louisiana Swamp Festival.

JAZZ IS BORN

In the early 1900s, African work chants and European and American folk music combined to create jazz. Jazz is America's first contribution to the world of music. It began partly in New Orleans. Louis Armstrong was born in New Orleans. He was one of the greatest jazz trumpeters of all time.

GUMBO

UR TAIL BIT HERE!

SAY IT RIGHT

Though New Orleans has a French and Spanish background, don't try to pronounce the street names with either accent. You will be identified immediately as an outsider. For example:

Chartres is pronounced CHAR ders.

Dumaine is pronounced DEW main.

Calliope is pronounced KEL ee ope.

13

Life in the Big Easy

For many years, New Orleans' main industries have been oil, shipping, and tourism. Before Hurricane Katrina, up to 10 million people visited New Orleans every year. In a city of about 400,000 people, 10 million visitors is quite spectacular!

The New Orleans French Quarter is on every visitor's must-see list. The French Quarter, or Vieux Carré (Old Square), is the original city. This is where the first French settlers turned some swampland into a town. The French Quarter is full of nineteenth-century buildings decorated with beautiful ironwork. Today, the buildings are private homes, stores, restaurants, hotels, and other businesses.

New Orleans' main industries are:

- oil
- shipping
- tourism

Just to the west of New Orleans is the world's longest over-water highway bridge. The Lake Pontchartrain Causeway spans 24 miles!

FAST FACT

Creole is a **controversial** and sometimes confusing term. At first, it referred to African slaves in America. Then it was applied to all pilgrims in the New World. By the nineteenth century, it often meant people native to New Orleans, especially those who spoke French. Some say the best definition is that anyone who claims to be a Creole is a Creole!

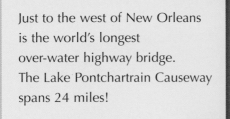

NEW ORLEANS

New Orleans Nicknames

Crescent City: for the shape of the land the city sits on

The Big Easy: possibly once the name of a dance hall; or simply a good name for a relaxed, laid-back city

The City That Care Forgot: possibly for the carefree attitude of its residents

MARDI GRAS AND CARNIVAL

New Orleans is famous for its carnival season. Carnival is an annual event. It begins on January 6, which is the Christian holiday called Epiphany or Twelfth Night. Carnival ends on the day before the Christian observance called Lent. It ends with the biggest party of all, called **Mardi Gras** Day. The weeks before Mardi Gras Day are filled with parades, costume balls, special foods, and happy celebrations. Hundreds of thousands of people gather in New Orleans to take part. On Mardi Gras Day, there is a final, huge parade. Costumed people on floats toss beads, cups, coins, and other small prizes into the cheering crowd.

We can't always be sure where a word comes from. For example, it is likely that *carnival* comes from Latin words that mean "to remove meat" – meat eating is restricted for 40 days after the celebration. But this explanation is difficult to prove.

All the Mardi Gras parades are put on by groups called krewes. Each krewe must hold a ball and take part in a parade with floats and bands.

DID YOU KNOW?

The official Mardi Gras colors are green, gold, and purple. Green stands for faith. Gold stands for power. Purple stands for justice.

Thousands of people crowd the streets for the Mardi Gras parade. It is a tradition to shout, "Throw me something, Mister," to people on floats.

WET AND WILD

A day trip out of New Orleans reminds visitors of the city's origins. There are rivers, bayous, and plenty of lakes. The wetlands are alive with alligators, birds, fish, deer, and beaver-like nutrias. Tall cypress trees loom out of the water, draped in moss.

In and around New Orleans, it is seldom very cold. In the winter, the temperature rarely falls below 48 °F. In the summer, the temperature rises to about 92 °F. However, the weather isn't always picture-perfect. Louisiana is one of the wettest states in the United States. New Orleans lies in the Mississippi **delta**, surrounded by water. When it's hot, the sun **evaporates** water from the waterways and ocean. Water **vapor** builds up in the air, creating one of the most notable things about the area – its humidity. To those not used to it, the air feels hot, damp, and thick.

Oh! I just misread the word *reminds*. I thought it was *remains*. But as I continued to read, it didn't make sense. So I went back and reread the sentence, and the word was obviously *reminds*.

Park rangers and other officials often travel by air boat. These fast-moving boats have one big propeller. The flat bottoms on the boats allow them to speed over shallow water. These rangers are releasing a captive-bred alligator.

SHOCKER

The air in New Orleans is so humid that people have reported waking up to find mold in their shoes.

Nutrias are large **rodents**. They live by swamps, lakes, and rivers. Nutrias were introduced to Louisiana from South America. They are sometimes seen as pests because they eat water plants.

THE SINKING CITY

Since 1930, about one million acres of wetlands have been destroyed in southern Louisiana. Oil drilling, underground pipelines, construction, and coastal **erosion** are mostly to blame. These actions have led to an actual sinking of New Orleans. In the 1700s, New Orleans was slightly above sea level. Today, it is 6 to 11 feet below sea level.

The wetlands originally provided protection for New Orleans against floodwaters. Wetlands act like giant sponges, soaking up excess floodwaters and releasing them slowly. Because of its warm waters, the Gulf of Mexico is a regular entry point for tropical storms and hurricanes. Coastal communities have built flood walls and **levees** for protection from high waves and rising water levels. But sometimes seawalls and levees fail.

After Hurricane Katrina, helicopters dropped sandbags to temporarily shore up broken levees in New Orleans.

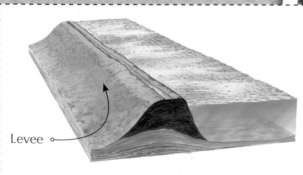

Levee

Levees work by blocking water with a raised bank of land or a wall.

SHOCKER

By 2005, Louisiana was losing a football-sized chunk of wetlands every 38 minutes.

Effect:
- New Orleans has been sinking.

Causes:
- underground pipelines
- drilling for oil
- construction
- coastal erosion

New Orleans buries its dead above ground. Water flows just below ground, so early settlers quickly discovered that buried caskets float away!

Hurricane Betsy hit New Orleans in 1965. Many families lost their homes. It was the first U.S. hurricane to cause more than $1 billion in damage. It was nicknamed "Billion-dollar Betsy."

21

Hurricane!

As Hurricane Katrina brewed, swirled, and raged in the Caribbean, the people of New Orleans began to react. Some immediately packed up and moved to higher ground. Some planned a Katrina-themed party. Many people didn't want to be bothered with **evacuating**. They thought the storm might miss New Orleans. Others had no way to leave, even if they wanted to.

On Sunday, August 28, 2005, a hush settled over the city. No birds sang. No stray cats meowed in the alleyways. Looking back, people realized this was a sign that something bad was about to happen. Animals have shown an instinct for evacuation before natural disasters, such as hurricanes and earthquakes. But for those not paying attention, the National Weather Service posted an unusually dramatic bulletin at 10:11 A.M. that day. It jolted many more people into leaving the area.

Oh, I already know something about that hurricane. So I should be able to make some good connections. These pages will help me get a better understanding of what it was like for the people who lived there.

22

DEVASTATING DAMAGE EXPECTED

THE NATIONAL WEATHER SERVICE
"HURRICANE KATRINA … A MOST POWERFUL HURRICANE WITH UNPRECEDENTED STRENGTH … MOST OF THE AREA WILL BE UNINHABITABLE FOR WEEKS, PERHAPS LONGER. AT LEAST ONE HALF OF WELL-CONSTRUCTED HOMES WILL HAVE ROOF AND WALL FAILURE … THE MAJORITY OF INDUSTRIAL BUILDINGS WILL BECOME NONFUNCTIONAL … HIGH-RISE OFFICE AND APARTMENT BUILDINGS WILL SWAY DANGEROUSLY … ALL WINDOWS WILL BLOW OUT … POWER OUTAGES WILL LAST FOR WEEKS … WATER SHORTAGES WILL MAKE HUMAN SUFFERING INCREDIBLE BY MODERN STANDARDS … DO NOT VENTURE OUTSIDE!"

On August 28, 2005, traffic on the interstate highway leaving downtown New Orleans was soon jammed. On some roads, traffic was later allowed to exit the city on both sides of the road.

SHOCKER
Sharks, elephants, and many other animals have abandoned an area right before a natural disaster. Scientists hope someday to be able to predict disasters merely by watching animal behavior!

The hole in the middle of a hurricane is its "eye." Surrounding the eye is the fiercest part of the storm.

KATRINA STRIKES

On Monday, August 29, 2005, the hurricane that everyone feared arrived. With winds reaching 180 miles per hour, Katrina roared and then attacked New Orleans. Winds spun store signs like pinwheels. Roofs, wood, and metal peeled off homes and businesses. Windows broke. Cars, boats, refrigerators, and TVs flew as if pitched like baseballs. Trees were stripped of leaves. Telephone and electric wires snapped, then hissed and sparked.

SHOCKER

One of the most common injuries during Katrina was red, raw hands with most of the skin ripped off. This happened because those who survived the rushing waters often did so by clinging to a tree branch.

At once, a stretch of flood wall along the Mississippi River collapsed. Rising waters rushed into the city. A flood wall along Lake Pontchartrain also crumbled. The lake, already higher than sea level, easily filled about 80 percent of low-lying New Orleans. Every person still in the city was in danger. Water, mud, and sewage rushed down streets. It rose higher and higher inside homes, schools, and businesses. It was as if a giant bucket of dirty water had been dumped over the city.

Some people escaped onto rooftops. They hoped that helicopters would rescue them from rising water.

Volunteers like this man helped to rescue people after Katrina. The U.S. Coast Guard alone saved more than 22,000 people after the hurricane.

DID YOU KNOW?

More than 1,800 people are known to have died from the storm. Many others were not found. It is estimated that 160,000 homes needed to be torn down and rebuilt. About 38,000 historic structures were damaged. Some were beyond repair. Losses were estimated to exceed $100 billion.

25

CLEANING UP

Once any stranded people were evacuated, the clean-up operation began. New Orleans was a toxic gumbo of brown water full of sewage, garbage, and other dangerous materials. Homes, belongings, and businesses had been torn apart and soaked in this sewage soup. Even as the water drained from the city, nearly everything was wet, ruined, and moldy. The stink was overpowering.

Though response was slower than it should have been, help soon arrived. The Red Cross and others tended to the sick and injured. Volunteers came from churches and other organizations. They brought supplies and started the clean-up. Professionals from all over the United States volunteered their services as doctors, counselors, builders, and so on. Some people came to help wild animals and stranded pets.

Aisha Turner was housed in a shelter with her mom and sister. She looked through donated clothes for something to wear to school.

Many rescued pets were flown to Los Angeles. There, they were taken care of. When possible, they were reunited with their owners. Others went to new homes.

SHOCKER

Before Katrina hit, officials at the New Orleans aquarium killed all the aquarium's piranhas. Piranhas are vicious meat-eaters that have been known to attack people. The officials feared that the piranhas might escape during the hurricane and breed in the Mississippi River.

The Smith family were able to clean up their yard a year after the hurricane.

DOWN THE DRAIN

It took about two months to drain the city of the water from Hurricanes Katrina and Rita. Rita was a slightly weaker hurricane that followed less than a month after Katrina.

New Orleans Today

On a New Orleans summer day, leaving the comfort of an air-conditioned room or store may give your body a jolt. The summer air hits you like hot air rushing out of an open oven door. On a walk through the French Quarter, you see that New Orleans is recovering from the storms of 2005. Levees and flood walls are repaired and strengthened. Homes and businesses lost during the storm are being rebuilt. The city's welcome mat is out. New Orleans wants and needs visitors.

Other parts of the city still need a great deal of work. Some areas are still in pieces. Some people doubt whether rebuilding is wise. Others are passionate about rebuilding their city. They are working toward better ways to protect the city they love.

These new floodgates were installed along the London Avenue Canal. The original floodgate gave way during the hurricane.

SHOCKER

Some scientists predict that the city of New Orleans will one day be totally under the water, like the mythical lost city of Atlantis.

EVACUATE NOW!

New Orleans has created a new evacuation plan. Plans have been made to ensure that all citizens can evacuate safely, even if they do not own a car.

HURRICANE EVACUATION ROUTE

FOR INFORMATION TUNE RADIO TO

870 AM
101.9 FM

Slightly more than five months after Katrina, the determined survivors brought Mardi Gras back to the streets of New Orleans. Numbers were down, but people celebrated more than ever.

The city of New Orleans is being rebuilt. New, stronger seawalls will help protect the city. However, New Orleans is still below sea level and still at risk of damage from floods and hurricanes. The wetlands are still being damaged. The Atlantic Ocean seems to be in a very active cycle of producing hurricanes.

WHAT DO YOU THINK?

Should we rebuild New Orleans, or should the citizens move to places less at risk from flooding?

PRO

Many people love New Orleans. It is where their families come from. Their friends live there. They love the city's unique culture. We should spend money restoring the wetlands so that the city will be protected naturally. This will help the environment too.

Some people argue that it makes no sense to rebuild an area that can be destroyed again so easily. Others believe it is dangerous to risk people's lives by welcoming them back to rebuild. Some families have chosen not to return. Others are determined to make their city a better, safer place for the future.

CON

The risk of another hurricane is too great. Perhaps we should rebuild the city farther inland, where it will be above sea level. In the long run, this may be safer and cost less.

Go to **www.timeforkids.com/ kids** and type in the search words *New Orleans* to read more about New Orleans.

GLOSSARY

controversial giving rise to disagreement or argument

crescent a curved shape similar to the moon when it is just a sliver in the sky

delta a wide area where a river deposits mud, sand, and pebbles, just before it meets the sea

erosion the wearing away, usually of land, by forces of wind or water

evacuate to leave a place because it may be too dangerous to stay there

evaporate to change from a liquid to a gas

humid having a large amount of water vapor in the air; humid air can feel damp and thick

inhabitant a person who lives in a place

integrated including people of different racial or ethnic groups

ironically with irony; when the outcome is very different from what was expected or planned

pungent strong and sharp; usually used about a taste or smell

rodent a mammal with sharp front teeth that it uses for gnawing – for example, a squirrel or a rat

vapor a gas made up of something that is usually liquid or solid at normal temperatures

INDEX